PIANO SOLO

JAZZY
CHRISTMAS TUNES

10 SPICY SETTINGS BY CRAIG CURRY

ISBN 978-1-4950-6892-8

7777 W. BLUEMOUND RD. P.O. BOX 13819 MILWAUKEE, WI 53213

Visit Hal Leonard Online at
www.halleonard.com

BABY, IT'S COLD OUTSIDE
from the Motion Picture NEPTUNE'S DAUGHTER

By FRANK LOESSER
Arranged by Craig Curry

DO YOU HEAR WHAT I HEAR

Words and Music by NOEL REGNEY
and GLORIA SHAYNE
Arranged by Craig Curry

I WONDER AS I WANDER

By JOHN JACOB NILES
Arranged by Craig Curry

FELIZ NAVIDAD

Music and Lyrics by JOSÉ FELICIANO
Arranged by Craig Curry

FROSTY THE SNOW MAN

Words and Music by STEVE NELSON
and JACK ROLLINS
Arranged by Craig Curry

A HOLLY JOLLY CHRISTMAS

Music and Lyrics by JOHNNY MARKS
Arranged by Craig Curry

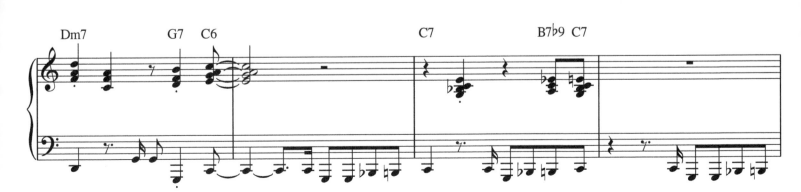

JINGLE BELL ROCK

Words and Music by JOE BEAL
and JIM BOOTHE
Arranged by Craig Curry

MARY, DID YOU KNOW?

Words and Music by MARK LOWRY
and BUDDY GREENE
Arranged by Craig Curry

30

WHITE CHRISTMAS

from the Motion Picture Irving Berlin's HOLIDAY INN

Words and Music by IRVING BERLIN
Arranged by Craig Curry

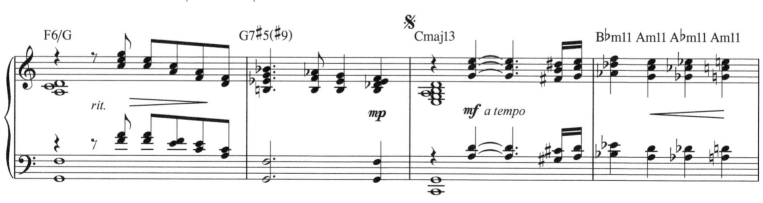

34

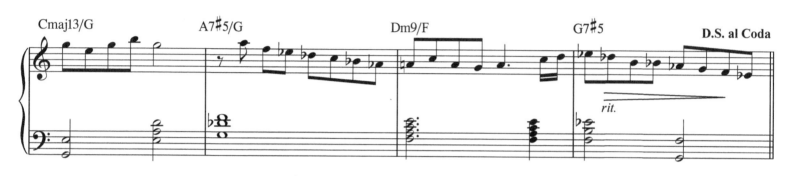

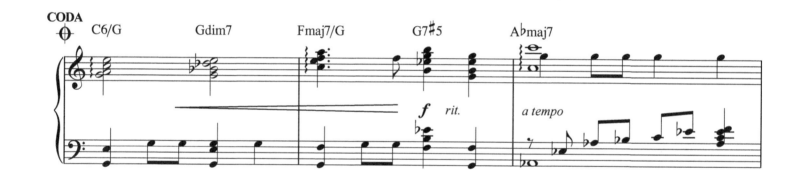

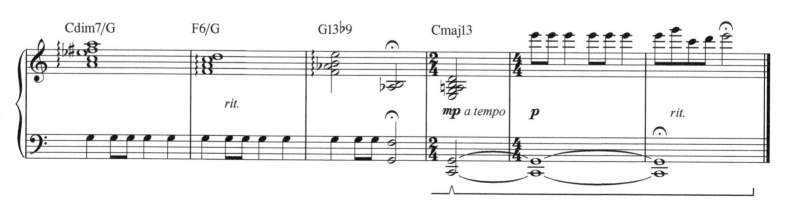

THE LITTLE DRUMMER BOY

Words and Music by HARRY SIMEONE,
HENRY ONORATI and KATHERINE DAVIS
Arranged by Craig Curry

jazz piano solos series

Each volume features exciting new arrangements with chord symbols of the songs which helped define a style.

vol. 1 miles davis
00306521................$19.99

vol. 2 jazz blues
00306522................$17.99

vol. 3 latin jazz
00310621................$16.99

vol. 4 bebop jazz
00310709................$16.99

vol. 5 cool jazz
00310710................$16.99

vol. 6 hard bop
00323507................$16.99

vol. 7 smooth jazz
00310727................$16.99

vol. 8 jazz pop
00311786................$17.99

vol. 9 duke ellington
00311787................$17.99

vol. 10 jazz ballads
00311788................$17.99

vol. 11 soul jazz
00311789................$17.99

vol. 12 swinging jazz
00311797................$17.99

vol. 13 jazz gems
00311899................$16.99

vol. 14 jazz classics
00311900................$16.99

vol. 15 bossa nova
00311906................$17.99

vol. 16 disney
00312121................$17.99

vol. 17 antonio carlos jobim
00312122................$17.99

vol. 18 modern jazz quartet
00307270................$16.99

vol. 19 bill evans
00307273................$19.99

vol. 20 gypsy jazz
00307289................$16.99

vol. 21 new orleans
00312169................$16.99

vol. 22 classic jazz
00001529................$17.99

vol. 23 jazz for lovers
00312548................$16.99

vol. 24 john coltrane
00307395................$17.99

vol. 25 christmas songs
00101790................$17.99

vol. 26 george gershwin
00103353................$17.99

vol. 27 late night jazz
00312547................$17.99

vol. 28 the beatles
00119302................$19.99

vol. 29 elton john
00120968................$19.99

vol. 30 cole porter
00123364................$17.99

vol. 31 cocktail piano
00123366................$17.99

vol. 32 johnny mercer
00123367................$16.99

vol. 33 gospel
00127079................$17.99

vol. 34 horace silver
00139633................$16.99

vol. 35 stride piano
00139685................$17.99

vol. 36 broadway jazz
00144365................$17.99

vol. 37 silver screen jazz
00144366................$16.99

vol. 38 henry mancini
00146382................$16.99

vol. 39 sacred christmas carols
00147678................$17.99

vol. 40 charlie parker
00149089................$16.99

vol. 41 pop standards
00153656................$16.99

vol. 42 dave brubeck
00154634................$16.99

vol. 43 candlelight jazz
00154901................$17.99

vol. 44 jazz standards
00160856................$17.99

vol. 45 christmas standards
00172024................$17.99

vol. 46 cocktail jazz
00172025................$17.99

vol. 47 hymns
00172026................$17.99

vol. 48 blue skies & other irving berlin songs
00197873................$16.99

vol. 49 thelonious monk
00232767................$16.99

vol. 50 best smooth jazz
00233277................$16.99

vol. 51 disney favorites
00233315................$16.99

vol. 52 bebop classics
00234075................$16.99

vol. 53 jazz-rock
00256715................$16.99

vol. 54 jazz fusion
00256716................$16.99

vol. 55 ragtime
00274961................$16.99

vol. 56 pop ballads
00274962................$16.99

vol. 57 pat metheny
00277058................$17.99

vol. 58 big band era
00284837................$17.99

vol. 59 west coast jazz
00290792................$17.99

vol. 60 boogie woogie
00363280................$17.99

vol. 61 christmas classics
00367872................$17.99

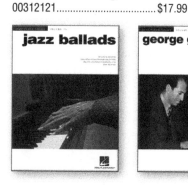

HAL•LEONARD®
View songlists and order online from your favorite music retailer at
www.halleonard.com

0621
Prices, contents & availability subject to change without notice. 427